# TRANSLATE

**Translated Language Learning**

# The Nightingale and the Rose

ナイチンゲールとバラ

Oscar Wilde

English / 日本語

Copyright © 2023 Tranzlaty
All rights reserved.
ISBN: 978-1-83566-009-6
Original text by Oscar Wilde
**The Nightingale and the Rose**
Written in 1888 in English
**www.tranzlaty.com**

# The Nightingale and the Rose
ナイチンゲールとバラ

'She said that she would dance with me if I brought her red roses'
「赤いバラを持ってきたら一緒に踊るって言ってたよ」
'but in all my garden there is no red rose' cried the young Student
「でも、うちの庭には赤いバラがないんだよ」と若い生徒は叫びました
from her nest in the holm-oak tree the nightingale heard him
セイヨウヒイラギガシの木の巣から、ナイチンゲールは彼の声を聞きました
and she looked out through the leaves, and wondered
そして、葉の間から外を眺め、不思議に思いました

'No red rose in all my garden!' he cried
「庭に赤いバラがいない!」と彼は叫びました
and his beautiful eyes filled with tears
そして、その美しい瞳には涙があふれていた
'On what little things does happiness depend!'
「幸せはどんな些細なことで決まるのか!」
'I have read all that the wise men have written'
「わたしは賢者たちの書いたものを全部読んだ」
'all the secrets of philosophy are mine'
「哲学の秘密はすべて私のもの」
'yet for want of a red rose my life is made wretched'
「しかし、赤い薔薇が欲しくて、私の人生は惨めなものになっている」

'Here at last is a true lover,' said the nightingale
「とうとう本当の恋人が来た」とナイチンゲールは言いました
'Night after night have I sung of him, though I knew him not'
「夜な夜な、わたしは彼のことを歌った。彼を知らなかったのに」
'Night after night have I told his story to the stars'
「夜な夜な、私は彼の物語を星々に語ってきた」

'and now I see him'
「そして今、私は彼に会う」

'His hair is as dark as the hyacinth-blossom'
「彼の髪はヒヤシンスの花のように暗い」
'and his lips are as red as the rose of his desire'
「そして彼の唇は彼の欲望の薔薇のように赤い」
'but passion has made his face like pale Ivory'
「しかし、情熱は彼の顔を青白い象牙のようにした」
'and sorrow has set her seal upon his brow'
「そして、悲しみが彼の額に封印をした」

'The Prince has organized a ball tomorrow,' said the young student
「王子様が明日舞踏会を企画したのよ」と若い生徒は言いました
'and my love will be there'
「そして私の愛はそこにある」
'If I bring her a red rose, she will dance with me'
「赤いバラを持ってきたら、一緒に踊ってくれる」
'If I bring her a red rose, I will hold her in my arms'
「赤いバラを持ってきたら、抱きしめてあげる」
'and she will lean her head upon my shoulder'
「そして、彼女は私の肩に頭をもたせかけるでしょう」
'and her hand will be clasped in mine'
「そうすれば、彼女の手は私の手で握りしめられるだろう」

'But there is no red rose in my garden'
「でも、庭には赤いバラがない」
'so I will sit lonely'
「だから私は孤独に座る」
'and she will go past me'
「そして、彼女は私を通り過ぎるでしょう」
'She will have no heed of me'
「あの子は私のことを気にかけてくれない」
'and my heart will break'
「そして私の心は壊れるだろう」

'Here indeed is the true lover,' said the nightingale
「ほんとうの恋人がここにいる」とナイチンゲールは言いました
'What I sing of he suffers'
「私が歌う彼の苦しみ」
'what is joy to me is pain to him'
「私にとっての喜びは、彼にとっての痛みである」
'Surely love is a wonderful thing'
「愛は確かに素晴らしいもの」
'love is more precious than emeralds'
「愛はエメラルドよりも尊い」

'and love is dearer than fine opals'
「そして愛は上質なオパールよりも大切です」
'Pearls and pomegranates cannot buy love'
「真珠とザクロは愛を買えない」
'nor is love sold in the market-place'
「愛は市場で売られるものでもない」
'love can not be bought from merchants'
「愛は商人から買えない」
'nor can love be weighed on a balance for gold'
「愛は金の天秤で量ることもできない」

'The musicians will sit in their gallery,' said the young student
「音楽家はギャラリーに座ってるんだよ」と若い学生は言った
'and they will play upon their stringed instruments'
「そして、彼らは弦楽器で演奏する」
'and my love will dance to the sound of the harp'
「そして私の愛はハープの音に合わせて踊る」
'and she will dance to the sound of the violin'
「そして彼女はバイオリンの音に合わせて踊るだろう」
'She will dance so lightly her feet won't touch the floor'
「足が床につかないほど軽やかに踊る」

'and the courtiers will throng round her'
「廷臣たちは彼女の周りに群がるだろう」

'but she will not dance with me'
「しかし、彼女は私と踊らない」
'because I have no red rose to give her'
「彼女にあげる赤いバラがないから」
he flung himself down on the grass
彼は草の上に身を投げ出した
and he buried his face in his hands and wept
そして両手で顔を埋めて泣いた


'Why is he weeping?' asked a little Green Lizard
「どうして泣いているの?」と小さな緑のトカゲが尋ねました
while he ran past with his tail in the air
尻尾を宙に浮かせて走り去りながら
'Why indeed?' said a Butterfly
「どうしてだい?」と蝶は言いました
while he was fluttering about after a sunbeam
太陽の光を浴びてバタバタしながら
'Why indeed?' whispered a daisy to his neighbour in a soft, low voice
「どうしてだい?」と、ヒナギクが隣人に小さな低い声でささやきました


'He is weeping for a red rose,' said the nightingale
「赤いバラが欲しくて泣いているんだ」とナイチンゲールは言いました
'For a red rose!?' they exclaimed
「赤い薔薇に!?」と彼らは叫んだ
'how very ridiculous!'
「なんてばかばかしいんだ!」
and the little Lizard, who was something of a cynic, laughed outright
そして、皮肉屋のような小さなトカゲは、あからさまに笑いました


But the nightingale understood the secret of the student's sorrow

しかし、ナイチンゲールは生徒の悲しみの秘密を理解していました
and she sat silent in the oak-tree
そして彼女は樫の木に黙って座っていた
and she thought about the mystery of love
そして、彼女は愛の神秘について考えました
Suddenly she spread her brown wings
突然、彼女は茶色の翼を広げた
and she soared into the air
そして彼女は空中に舞い上がった

She passed through the grove like a shadow
彼女は影のように木立を通り抜けた
and like a shadow she sailed across the garden
そして影のように庭を横切った
In the centre of the garden was a beautiful rose-tree
庭の真ん中には美しいバラの木がありました
and when she saw the rose-tree, she flew over to it
そして、バラの木を見ると、そのところに飛んで行きました
and she perched upon a twig
そして彼女は小枝にとまりました

'Give me a red rose,' she cried
「赤い薔薇をちょうだい」と彼女は叫んだ
'give me a red rose and I will sing you my sweetest song'
「赤いバラをくれれば、私の最も甘い歌を歌ってあげる」
But the Tree shook its head
しかし、木は首を横に振った
'My roses are white,' the rose-tree answered
「ぼくの薔薇は白いよ」と薔薇の木は答えました

'as white as the foam of the sea'
「海の泡のように白い」
'and whiter than the snow upon the mountain'
「山の雪よりも白い」
'But go to my brother who grows round the old sun-dial'

「でも、古い日時計の周りをぐるぐる回っている兄のところに行ってみよう」
'perhaps he will give you what you want'
「もしかしたら、彼はあなたが望むものを与えてくれるかもしれません」

So the nightingale flew over to his brother
それでナイチンゲールは弟のところに飛んでいきました
the rose-tree growing round the old sun-dial
古い日時計の周りに生えている薔薇の木
'Give me a red rose,' she cried
「赤い薔薇をちょうだい」と彼女は叫んだ
'give me a red rose and I will sing you my sweetest song'
「赤いバラをくれれば、私の最も甘い歌を歌ってあげる」
But the rose-tree shook its head
しかし、薔薇の木は首を横に振った
'My roses are yellow,' the rose-tree answered
「ぼくの薔薇は黄色だよ」と薔薇の木は答えました

'as yellow as the hair of a mermaid'
「人魚の髪の毛のように黄色い」
'and yellower than the daffodil that blooms in the meadow'
「草原に咲く水仙よりも黄色い」
'before the mower comes with his scythe'
「芝刈り機が鎌を持って来る前に」
'but go to my brother who grows beneath the student's window'
「でも、生徒の窓の下に生えているお兄ちゃんのところに行って」
'and perhaps he will give you what you want'
「そして、もしかしたら、あなたが望むものを与えてくれるかもしれません」

So the nightingale flew over to his brother
それでナイチンゲールは弟のところに飛んでいきました
the rose-tree growing beneath the student's window
生徒の窓の下に生えている薔薇の木

'give me a red rose,' she cried
「赤いバラをちょうだい」と彼女は叫んだ
'give me a red rose and I will sing you my sweetest song'
「赤いバラをくれれば、私の最も甘い歌を歌ってあげる」
But the rose-tree shook its head
しかし、薔薇の木は首を横に振った

'My roses are red,' the rose-tree answered
「ぼくの薔薇は赤いよ」と薔薇の木は答えました
'as red as the feet of the dove'
「鳩の足のように赤い」
'and redder than the great fans of coral'
「そして、珊瑚の大ファンよりも赤い」
'the corals that sway in the ocean-cavern'
「海の洞窟で揺れる珊瑚」

'But the winter has chilled my veins'
「しかし、冬は私の血管を冷やした」
'and the frost has nipped my buds'
「霜がつぼみを摘んでしまった」
'and the storm has broken my branches'
「嵐が私の枝を折った」
'and I shall have no roses at all this year'
「今年はバラの花がまったく咲かない」

'One red rose is all I want,' cried the nightingale
「赤いバラが一本欲しいだけだよ」とナイチンゲールは叫びました
'Is there no way by which I can get it?'
「どうやって手に入れるのか?」
'There is a way' answered the rose-tree'
「道はある」と薔薇の木は答えました。
'but it is so terrible that I dare not tell you'
「しかし、それはあまりにひどいので、あえて言わない」
'Tell it to me' said the nightingale
「教えてくれ」とナイチンゲールは言いました
'I am not afraid'
「怖くない」

'If you want a red rose,' said the rose-tree
「赤い薔薇が欲しかったら」と薔薇の木は言いました
'if you want a red rose you must build the rose out of music'
「赤い薔薇が欲しければ、音楽から薔薇を作らなければならない」
'while the moonlight shines upon you'
「月明かりがあなたを照らしながら」
'and you must stain the rose with your own heart's blood'
「そして、あなたは自分の心の血で薔薇を汚さなければなりません」

'You must sing to me with your breast against a thorn'
「棘に胸を当てて歌わねばならぬ」
'All night long you must sing to me'
「一晩中、あなたは私に歌わなければならない」
'the thorn must pierce your heart'
「棘は君の心を突き刺さなければならない」
'your life-blood must flow into my veins'
「お前の生命の血は俺の血管に流れ込むに違いない」
'and your life-blood must become my own'
「そして、あなたの生命線は私のものになるに違いない」

'Death is a high price to pay for a red rose,' cried the nightingale
「死は赤いバラに払う高い代償だ」とナイチンゲールは叫びました
'life is very dear to all'
「人生はすべての人にとってとても大切なものです」
'It is pleasant to sit in the green wood'
「緑の森に座るのが楽しい」
'it is nice to watch the sun in his chariot of gold'
「金の戦車で太陽を見るのはいいことだ」
'and it is nice to watch the moon in her chariot of pearl'
「真珠の戦車で月を見るのはいいわね」

'sweet is the scent of the hawthorn'
「サンザシの香りは甘い」

'sweet are the bluebells that hide in the valley'
「渓谷に隠れるブルーベルは甘い」
'and sweet is the heather that blows on the hill'
「そして、丘に吹くヒースは甘い」
'Yet love is better than life'
「しかし、愛は命にまさる」

'and what is the heart of a bird compared to the heart of a man?'
「鳥の心は、人間の心と比べて何でしょうか?」
So she spread her brown wings for flight
そこで彼女は茶色の翼を広げて飛翔した
and she soared into the air
そして彼女は空中に舞い上がった
She swept over the garden like a shadow
彼女は影のように庭を覆った
and like a shadow she sailed through the grove
そして影のように、彼女は木立の中を航海した

The young Student was still lying in the garden
若い生徒はまだ庭に横たわっていました
and his tears were not yet dry in his beautiful eyes
そして、その美しい瞳にはまだ涙が乾いていなかった
'Be happy,' cried the nightingale
「幸せになりなさい」とナイチンゲールは叫びました
'you shall have your red rose'
「赤い薔薇をもらおう」
'I will make your rose out of music'
「私はあなたのバラを音楽から作ります」
'while the moonlight shines upon me'
「月明かりが私を照らしながら」

'and I will stain your rose with my own heart's blood'
「そして、私はあなたの薔薇を私の心の血で汚します」
'All that I ask of you in return is that you will be a true lover'
「私があなたに求めるのは、あなたが真の恋人になることだけです」

'because love is wiser than Philosophy, though she is wise'
「愛は哲学よりも賢いからだ。愛は賢明であるが」
'and love is mightier than power, though he is mighty'
「そして、愛は力よりも強大である。彼は強大であるが」

'flame-coloured are his wings'
「炎の色は彼の翼である」
'and coloured like flame is his body'
「そして、彼の体は炎のように色づいている」
'His lips are as sweet as honey'
「彼の唇は蜂蜜のように甘い」
'and his breath is like frankincense'
「そして、彼の息は乳香のようだ」

The Student looked up from the grass
生徒は草むらから顔を上げた
and he listened to the nightingale
そして彼はナイチンゲールに耳を傾けました
but he could not understand what she was saying
しかし、彼は彼女が何を言っているのか理解できませんでした
because he only knew what he had read in books
なぜなら、彼は本で読んだことしか知らなかったからです
But the Oak-tree understood, and he felt sad
しかし、樫の木は理解し、悲しくなりました

he was very fond of the little nightingale
彼は小さなナイチンゲールがとても好きでした
because she had built her nest in his branches
なぜなら、彼女は彼の枝に巣を作ったからです
'Sing one last song for me,' he whispered
「最後の歌を歌ってくれ」と彼はささやいた
'I shall feel very lonely when you are gone'
「あなたがいなくなったら、とても寂しい思いをします」
So the nightingale sang to the Oak-tree
それでナイチンゲールは樫の木に向かって歌いました
and her voice was like water bubbling from a silver jar
その声は銀の壺から泡立つ水のようだった

When she had finished her song the student got up
彼女が歌い終えると、生徒は立ち上がった
and he pulled out a note-book
そして彼は一冊のメモ帳を取り出した
and he found a lead-pencil in his pocket
そして、ポケットの中に鉛筆を見つけました
'She has form,' he said to himself
「あの子には形がある」と彼は自分に言い聞かせた
'that she has form cannot be denied to her'
「彼女が形を持っていることは、彼女にとって否定できない」
'but does she have feeling?'
「でも、あの子には感情があるの?」
'I am afraid she has no feeling'
「あの子には感情がないんじゃないかしら」

'In fact, she is like most artists'
「実際、彼女はほとんどのアーティストと同じです」
'she is all style, without any sincerity'
「彼女はすべてスタイルで、誠実さがない」
'She would not sacrifice herself for others'
「他人のために自分を犠牲にしたりはしない」
'She thinks merely of music'
「彼女は音楽のことしか考えていない」
'and everybody knows that the arts are selfish'
「そして、芸術が利己的であることは誰もが知っている」

'Still, it must be admitted that she has some beautiful notes'
「それでも、彼女が美しい音符を持っていることは認めざるを得ません」
'it's a pity her song does not mean anything'
「彼女の歌が何の意味も持たないのは残念だ」
'and it's a pity her song is not useful'
「彼女の歌が役に立たないのは残念だ」
And he went into his room
そして彼は自分の部屋に入っていった
and he lay down on his little pallet-bed
そして、小さなパレットベッドに横たわりました

and he began to think of his love until he fell asleep
そして、眠りにつくまで愛のことを考え始めました

And when the moon shone in the heavens the nightingale flew to the Rose-tree
そして、月が天に輝くと、ナイチンゲールはバラの木に飛んでいきました
and she set her breast against the thorn
そして、乳房を棘に当てた
All night long she sang with her breast against the thorn
一晩中、彼女は胸を棘に当てて歌いました
and the cold crystal Moon leaned down and listened
冷たい水晶の月は身を乗り出して耳を傾けた
All night long she sang
一晩中、彼女は歌った
and the thorn went deeper and deeper into her breast
そして、棘は彼女の胸にどんどん深く入り込んでいきました
and her life-blood ebbed away from her
そして彼女の生命の血は彼女から消えていった

First she sang of the birth of love in the heart of a boy and a girl
まず、彼女は男の子と女の子の心に愛が生まれることを歌った
And on the topmost branch of the rose-tree there blossomed a marvellous rose
そして、バラの木の一番上の枝に、素晴らしいバラの花が咲いていました
petal followed petal, as song followed song
花びらが花びらに続き、歌が歌に続いたように
At first the rose was still pale
最初、薔薇はまだ青白かった

as pale as the mist that hangs over the river
川に漂う霧のように青白い
as pale as the feet of the morning
朝の足のように青白い
and as silver as the wings of dawn

夜明けの翼のように銀色に
As pale the shadow of a rose in a mirror of silver
銀の鏡に映る薔薇の影のように淡い
as pale as the shadow of a rose in a pool of water
水たまりに浮かぶ薔薇の影のように青白く

But the Tree cried to the nightingale;
しかし、木はナイチンゲールに叫びました。
'Press closer, little nightingale, or the day will come before the rose is finished'
「もっと近づいて、小さなナイチンゲール。さもないと、バラが咲く前に日が来てしまう」
So the nightingale pressed closer against the thorn
それでナイチンゲールは棘に近づきました
and her song grew louder and louder
そして彼女の歌はどんどん大きくなっていった
because she sang of the birth of passion in the soul of a man and a maid
なぜなら、彼女は男と女中の魂に情熱が生まれることを歌ったからだ

And the leaves of the rose flushed a delicate pink
そして、薔薇の葉は繊細なピンク色に紅潮しました
like the flush in the face of the bridegroom when he kisses the lips of the bride
花婿が花嫁の唇に接吻するときの顔の紅潮のように
But the thorn had not yet reached her heart
しかし、その棘はまだ彼女の心に届いていなかった
so the rose's heart remained white
薔薇の心は白いままだった
because only a nightingale's blood can crimson the heart of a rose
ナイチンゲールの血だけがバラの心臓を真紅に染めることができるからです

And the Tree cried to the nightingale;
そして木はナイチンゲールに叫びました。

'Press closer, little nightingale, or the day will come before the rose is finished'
「もっと近づいて、小さなナイチンゲール。さもないと、バラが咲く前に日が来てしまう」
So the nightingale pressed closer against the thorn
それでナイチンゲールは棘に近づきました
and the thorn touched her heart
そして棘が彼女の心に触れた
and a fierce pang of pain shot through her
そして激しい痛みが彼女を撃ち抜いた

Bitter, bitter was the pain
苦い、苦い痛みだった
and wilder and wilder grew her song
そして、彼女の歌はどんどん荒々しくなっていった
because she sang of the love that is perfected by death
なぜなら、彼女は死によって完成される愛を歌ったからだ
she sang of the love that does not die in life
彼女は人生で死なない愛を歌った
she sang of the love that does not die in the tomb
彼女は墓の中で死なない愛を歌った
And the marvellous rose became crimson like the rose of the eastern sky
そして、その素晴らしい薔薇は、東の空の薔薇のように真っ赤になりました
Crimson was the girdle of petals
クリムゾンは花びらの帯だった
as crimson as a ruby was the heart
ルビーのように深紅の心臓だった

But the nightingale's voice grew fainter
しかし、ナイチンゲールの声は次第に小さくなってきました
and her little wings began to beat
そして彼女の小さな翼が鼓動し始めた
and a film came over her eyes
そして、彼女の目にフィルムが浮かびました
fainter and fainter grew her song

彼女の歌はどんどん小さくなっていった
and she felt something choking her in her throat
そして、喉に何かが詰まるのを感じた
then she gave one last burst of music
そして、彼女は最後の音楽を披露した

the white Moon heard it, and she forgot the dawn
白い月はそれを聞いて、夜明けを忘れた
and she lingered in the sky
そして彼女は空にとどまった
The red rose heard it
赤い薔薇はそれを聞いた
and the rose trembled with ecstasy
そして薔薇は恍惚に震えた
and the rose opened its petals to the cold morning air
そして、薔薇は冷たい朝の空気に花びらを開きました

Echo carried it to her purple cavern in the hills
エコーはそれを丘の紫色の洞窟に運んだ
and it woke the sleeping shepherds from their dreams
眠っている羊飼いたちを夢から目覚めさせた
It floated through the reeds of the river
それは川の葦の間を漂っていた
and the rivers carried its message to the sea
そして、川はそのメッセージを海に運びました

'Look, look!' cried the Tree
「見て、見て!」と木は叫びました
'the rose is finished now'
「薔薇はもう終わった」
but the nightingale made no answer
しかし、ナイチンゲールは何も答えませんでした
for she was lying dead in the long grass, with the thorn in her heart
彼女は長い草むらで死んで横たわっていて、心に棘が刺さっていたからである

And at noon the student opened his window and looked out
正午、生徒は窓を開けて外を見た
'What a wonderful piece of luck!' he cried
「なんて素晴らしい幸運なんだ!」と彼は叫びました
'here is a red rose!'
「ここに赤い薔薇がある!」
'I have never seen any rose like it'
「こんなバラは見たことがない」
'It is so beautiful that I am sure it has a long Latin name'
「とても美しいので、ラテン語の長い名前がついていると思います」
he leaned down and plucked the rose
彼は身を乗り出して薔薇を摘み取った
then he ran up to the professor's house with the rose in his hand
それから彼はバラを手に教授の家に駆け寄りました

The professor's daughter was sitting in the doorway
教授の娘は戸口に座っていた
she was winding blue silk on a reel
彼女は青い絹をリールに巻き上げていた
and her little dog was lying at her feet
そして、彼女の小さな犬が彼女の足元に横たわっていました
'You said that you would dance with me if I brought you a red rose'
「赤い薔薇を持ってきたら一緒に踊るって言ったでしょ」
'Here is the reddest rose in all the world'
「これが世界で一番赤いバラです」
'You will wear it tonight, next your heart'
「今夜は着るよ、君の心の次は」
'While we dance together it will tell you how I love you'
「一緒に踊っているうちに、私があなたを愛していることがわかる」

But the girl frowned
しかし少女は眉をひそめた
'I am afraid it will not go with my dress'

「ドレスに合わないのではないかと心配」
'Anyway, the Chamberlain's nephew sent me some real jewels'
「とにかく、侍従の甥が本物の宝石を送ってくれた」
'and everybody knows jewels cost more than flowers'
「そして、宝石は花よりも高価であることは誰もが知っています」
'Well, you are very ungrateful!' said the Student angrily
「まあ、お前は恩知らずだ!」と生徒は怒って言いました
and he threw the rose into the street
そして彼は薔薇を通りに投げ捨てた
and the rose fell into the gutter
そして薔薇は側溝に落ちた
and a cart-wheel ran over the rose
そして、カートホイールが薔薇の上を走りました

'Ungrateful!' said the girl
「恩知らず!」と娘は言いました
'Let me tell you this; you are very rude'
「これだけは言わせてください。あなたはとても失礼です」
'and who are you anyway? Only a Student!'
「それで、お前は一体何者なんだ?ただの生徒だ!」
'You don't even have silver buckles on your shoes'
「靴に銀のバックルすら付いていない」
'The Chamberlain's nephew has far nicer shoes'
「侍従の甥はずっといい靴を履いている」
and she got up from her chair and went into the house
そして椅子から立ち上がり、家の中へ入って行きました

'What a silly thing Love is,' said the Student, while he walked away
「愛とはなんて愚かなものなんだ」と生徒は言いながら立ち去りました
'love is not half as useful as Logic'
「愛は論理の半分も役に立たない」
'because it does not prove anything'
「何の証明にもならないから」

'Love always tells of things that won't happen'
「愛はいつも起こらないことを告げる」
'and love makes you believe things that are not true'
「そして愛はあなたに真実ではないことを信じさせる」
'In fact, love is quite unpractical'
「実際、愛はまったく現実的ではありません」

'in this age being practical is everything'
「今の時代は実用性がすべて」
'I shall go back to Philosophy and I will study Metaphysics'
「哲学に戻り、形而上学を勉強する」
So he returned to his room
それで彼は自分の部屋に戻った
and he pulled out a great dusty book
そして、埃まみれの大きな本を取り出しました
and he began to read
そして彼は読み始めた

**The End - 最後です**

www.ingramcontent.com/pod-product-compliance
Lightning Source LLC
Chambersburg PA
CBHW011955090526
44591CB00020B/2788